IMPROVING THE LANDSCAPE OF YOUR LIFE

IMPROVING THE LANDSCAPE OF YOUR LIFE

PETER BURWASH

TORCHLIGHT PUBLISHING

LOS ANGELES • DELHI

First Printing 1999

Cover design by Yamaraja Dasa
Interior design by Christopher Glenn / Glenn Graphics
Printed in the United States of America

Published simultaneously in the United States of America and Canada by Torchlight Publishing, Inc.

Library of Congress Cataloging-in-Publication Data

    Burwash, Peter.
        Improving the landscape of your life / by Peter Burwash
        p.   cm.
        ISBN 1-887089-15-2 (hardcover)
        I.   Success—Psychological aspects. 2. Conduct of life.
        I. Title.
        BF637.S8 B785   1999
        158.1—dc21   97-35309

Attention Colleges, Universities, Corporations, Associations and Professional Organizations: *Improving the Landscape of Your Life* is available at special discounts for bulk purchases for fund-raising or educational use. Special books, booklets, or excerpts can be created to suit your specific needs.

Torchlight Publishing, Inc.

For more information, contact the Publisher.
PO Box 52
Badger CA 93603
Email: torchlight @compuserve.com
www.torchlight.com

Dedication

To our youngest daughter, Skyler.
By adopting you,
I hope we improved
the landscape of your life.

Contents

Foreword

Anyone who knows me knows I like to read. In fact, I enjoy reading so much that I wrote two bestsellers myself!

Every once in a while, a really interesting read comes my way and strikes a chord. Peter Burwash has done just that. In this book, he offers a blend of practical wisdom and a depth of experience to teach us how to take charge in every aspect of our lives. He offers a solid foundation for understanding the human condition and improving personal effectiveness.

I haven't really known Peter very long, but I am certainly inspired by his personal convictions. He came into my life just recently to give me tennis lessons. I figure anybody who can take on my tennis game and improve it must have perserverance—talk about taking on an adverse situation and making it positive! This guy really acts on his word.

In this book, Peter humbly offers the reader a fresh and practical approach to integrating life responsibilities with personal values.

This is a man who really cares and who really wants to make a difference. And he does.

Lee Iacocca

Introduction

It is never too late to be what you might have been. It's amazing how many people, even in their 40s and 50s, have stopped learning...and stopped growing. It should be a life-long mission to be better today than we were yesterday. However, before embarking on the path to improvement, it's important to be aware of some of the hurdles ahead.

The biggest challenge we face today is that we have become a society of "instant everything." In fact, instant gratification isn't soon enough sometimes. We have lost the appreciation of struggle. Our patience and perseverance are limited. We channel surf our TVs. We spend years abusing our bodies with the wrong foods and drinks and then plunk ourselves down on the doctor's table and want an instant fix or repair job. We don't exercise for years and then want a quick weight loss within a week.

In addition to our instant-result mentality, we have become blind by the dazzling glitter of material opulence. Those who have lots of material possessions want more, and those who don't have them spend an inordinate amount of time craving what they don't have. It's a material jungle out there. Since the 1980s—in the Western world, in particular—it's been an era of greed. At one point in America, a shopping center was being completed every seven hours. In sports, salaries have escalated so much that many athletes are emotionally overwhelmed by making so much money at such a young age; they lose sight of reality.

What is fascinating about this marked pursuit of material possessions is that people genuinely believe that wealth, things and position will bring happiness. Instead, it just brings more bewilderment in their elusive search. Happiness is like a butterfly. If you try to catch it in your hands, it flies away. Yet if you turn your attention elsewhere, it will come and land on your shoulder. It is important to realize that happiness should not be our principal goal. In actuality, it is a byproduct of our efforts to make other people happy. Happiness truly belongs to those who live for others. The more you focus on helping others, the more you will come to see that kindness is directly linked to happiness.

Remember the perfect gift you bought for someone? You give it to them and you can hardly wait for them to open it. Yet, when you were the recipient, you often felt embarrassed or uncomfortable. Giving, whether it be a material gift or a gift of the heart, makes us happy.

In countries like America, where wealth is abundant, happiness can scarcely be found. America influences behavior patterns globally. And one of our worst exports has been the illusions created by the world of advertising. We are in a society that is constantly selling something new to us. Advertising often creates an appearance of need where none exists. Advertising has its place, but most ads promise that our life will be happier if we buy their particular product. What kind of happiness is that? It is amazing that this avalanche of commercials can inflate trivial items like deodorant and shampoo into something extremely important. Our modern society has a high need for excitement and stimulation, so days and weeks are spent putting together slick, fast-paced ads with mood music to lure us in. These ads perpetuate our desire to have more. Ads work to persuade one that happiness lies in escalating the consumption of material goods. Today's electronic world stirs up our desires faster, although craving more is not new or unique to this era. It has always been a part of human nature to want more.

When people are asked what the goal of life is, a large percentage answer "to be happy." Yet when asked what will make them happier, so many people focus on themselves and their needs. What you can become is much more important than what you can accumulate. By realizing that our focus should be directed toward others to become happy, we will see a radical shift in how we feel inside. There is no question that the best way to make yourself happy is to make someone else happy. The happiest people don't necessarily have the best of everything, but they almost always make something good out of what happens. If you take this approach, you will see a marked difference in what the landscape of your life looks like. The most important thing we can do to improve the landscape of our life is to understand true happiness.

I remember the first year of our first child. I had not wanted children. I was very content traveling all over the world helping people improve their tennis game, or their health or leadership skills. I could not see the value of spending such an inordinate amount of time (as I then perceived it) on one individual. The commitment of time, energy and emotion seemed out of balance.

However, because I have always felt very responsible to whatever I was involved in, I chipped in right from the beginning in taking care of our child. Within twenty-four hours I was changing diapers, doing the feedings and all the time looking forward to teaching this little girl about life. About the end of the first year, I came to a startling realization. Raising a child is not so much about what you teach your child but, really what that child teaches you. Looking at life through a child's eyes is marvelous. After the light bulb went on, there was a surge of happiness that I hadn't experienced before. As I write this, I understand that the best part of my life is being "a Daddy" to my two daughters. The child truly is the father/mother of men.

What really happened? I became a student, a follower. I came to realize how much happier children are—how much more they smile. I entered the child's world of wonderment, enthusiasm and exploration.

We can't truly serve others unless we do a regular internal audit. Until we learn to change the world inside us, we will never be able to change the world outside. Every human being wants to change things in their life. Sometimes the changes aren't always for the better, such as those wrought by selfish lust. But desires for service spring from the transformative power of love.

The following twelve chapters in this book are independent of one another. You could read them in any order. You can prioritize them according to your needs or interests. They are, however, equally important in our quest to truly be happy and contribute.

A few years ago I attended a seminar by Rabbi Kushner, entitled "Plant a Tree, Have a Child and Write a Book." As a youngster I planted a lot of trees. And I now have two children. And this is my seventh book. But the information in the first six books was transferred from my head to paper. This book, *Improving the Landscape of Your Life*, is the first written from my heart. I feel that this is the spirit with which Rabbi Kushner spoke that day. I hope when you are finished with it you will be a better person. Let me know—my address is at the back.

Chapter One

Have the Courage to Change

We must be willing at any moment to sacrifice what we are for what we may become. And that takes courage. Whenever you see a company, a country, a family or an individual that has succeeded in making significant changes, there were some courageous decisions made. Every individual that has done something successful can look back and reflect on the times where their life took a different path. And a big part of that process was the courage to do it. We need courage to look at ourselves and change.

Look at the difference between children and adults. Children are full of hopes and dreams. They believe they can do almost anything when they grow up. They are free of so many hang-ups. Yet, as they get older, they start to question themselves. The dreams turn to doubts. The hopes turn to fears.

What happens to cause this transition? In a lot of cases, it is due to discouraging comments from family members, friends or teachers. If every person kept a diary of times when their dreams or hopes were verbally stonewalled, and if they had succumbed to these doubters, there wouldn't be any courageous success stories.

Amidst all the naysayers, there are always one or two individuals who can understand why you want to change and who can be your emotional cheerleaders. It is extremely helpful to have these people along as your companions or aides. But always remember that you are the one and only person that ultimately decides to change your destiny. Deciding to change and grow is the "architectural" stage. Actually doing it is the "construction" stage; once the "building" is underway, visualizing what the end result will look like will be much easier.

Sometimes we are thrust into a role where people say it was a courageous act. But if you talk to individuals who have saved someone from drowning or rescued someone from inside a burning house, they almost always observe, "I was just doing what anyone else would have done." When they get the accolades or their hero's medal, they are almost embarrassed at the recognition. Why? Because deep down they know they weren't really courageous; they just reacted, doing "what anyone else would have done."

Real courage is the prisoner in jail who makes the decision to turn his life around, whether he is there for life or being released soon. Real courage is to sit down with yourself, do some genuine introspection, and make the changes to improve your life so that you can improve others' lives. Real courage is being able to sit down with your spouse and admit you are wrong. Real courage is being able to say "I'm sorry" and feel it with your heart. Real courage is deciding to do what needs to get done, even though it isn't the popular path.

Life isn't easy. Too often it is human nature to follow the path of least resistance. What is critical if we want to improve our lives is to have the courage to struggle and sacrifice. One of the biggest mistakes of the post-1930s depression era was that those individuals who became parents did not want their kids to have to struggle like they did. They wanted to make things easier for their children. What we all need, however, is the experience of struggle. Adversity introduces one to who they really are.

For those of you who haven't had the courage to change your life: what are you afraid of? You know you'll improve and the end result will be better. But you are probably afraid of the process . . . the struggle. Take the battered wife. She wants out of the relationship desperately. She knows life will be better without the physical and emotional beatings. Yet she hangs on. Not because she wants to but because she is afraid of the process that she will have to go through to improve her life. We all have what are called our "desert" experiences . . . the times when our life feels very empty. The key is to not allow ourselves to be stranded in the desert.

If we all view struggle and sacrifice as positives, it will help us make a more courageous decision. When you talk to people who have had the courage to change, they almost all look back at the process itself as a genuine character-building experience.

Great champions in sports often visualize the final moment of their victory many years in advance. Why don't you do the same? Draw a picture or write an essay about what the new phase of your life will be like. Take some quiet time in a tranquil setting . . . all by yourself. Take a pencil and pad with you. Regardless of your literary or artistic capabilities, begin to outline your new "life," both in words and visually.

Recently, I spoke to a sixth-grade class at an all-girls' school. After the talk, the teacher asked each student to first write about what they had learned and, second, to DRAW what they had learned. Their efforts were presented to me in a bound booklet. What was amazing to me was how talented and perceptive the students were. But the real talent usually was only in one area. However, what was interesting was that what they wrote and what they drew complemented one another. Seldom did they draw what they wrote about or vice versa. What resulted was an expanded and diversified version of what they had learned.

One of the girls was quite touched about a story I told of three dolphins saving a lady who had been cast into shark-infested waters after she abandoned her sailboat when the stove had exploded. Two dolphins hoisted this lady out of the water while the third circled them to keep the sharks away, taking her many miles to safety. In her written communication, the schoolgirl described her passion and love for dolphins and how she wanted to save them from the numerous drift nets laid down by fishermen in our oceans. In her communication there was a determination and commitment to be helpful. Yet when she drew the experience, the artwork was full of color: blue water, sunshine, smiling dolphins—even the lady who was being saved had a smile on her face in spite of the terror of sharks all around her.

So in your efforts to draw and write about your new existence, do not limit the dream by saying you can't write or draw. Nobody is going to grade you on the result. JUST WRITE AND DRAW. Then put it in a safe place. After you have made the change, take it out—you'll be amazed at how close your dream actually comes to reality.

Commitment to dreams can definitely help us be more courageous. As Vince Lombardi, the former coach of the Green Bay

Packers and one of the best motivators of our century, says, "Give me desire and courage over talent, and I will give you a winner."

One night Don Gevirtz, former ambassador to the United States in Fiji, told me that he only wants two words on his tombstone: "HE GREW." What a wonderful tribute to his life.

And as an early explorer said, "You can't discover new oceans unless you have the courage to lose sight of the shore." It's time to set your sails.

Chapter Two

Make Health the Foundation
Of Your Life

Good health is the physical foundation to getting your life to a higher
plateau. It's pretty difficult to improve the
landscape of your life if you don't make the
commitment to a healthier life style. If you
can remember the last time you really felt ill,
and you were lying in bed, the last thing on
your mind was how you could help other people. When you are sick, almost the entire
focus is on you and your ailing body. We usually don't value our health until we lose it.

Being physically, mentally and emotionally healthy in today's society is not easy. Because of the enormous ecological devastation of our planet the last one hundred years, we have permanently altered our land, water and air. Couple this with the fact that so many more people are turning up the speed on the treadmill of their life. Go to any major city and people look like rats running through the day-to-day maze of life. In a recent study it was found that 94% of American adults say they use their free time not to relax, not to have fun—but to recuperate from working.

As well, two-income households have put time constraints on families. This has lead to more consumption of fat-laden, fast, convenient foods which are high in cholesterol and saturated fats. This generally leads to an overweight individual. And when you are overweight, it isn't just your insecurity that rises—it's hard work on your body.

When I was in Grade 7, I had a physical education teacher, John Chomay, who gave me one of my best life lessons. On Monday afternoon he had us do a series of our regular physical exercises against time. We recorded everything. On Tuesday morning when we got to school, he placed a five-pound belt on our bodies. This belt was to be kept on until after school. By the time we were to do our exercises that afternoon, we were exhausted. Our scores for the exercises were deplorable. Nobody came close to equaling their Monday output. At the end of the day he gathered us around. As we all sat staring up at him, he said, "Don't ever put on five pounds above your normal weight." Our young minds needed no further explanation. I never forgot Mr. Chomay's brilliant demonstration.

Today we put food and drink into our body that genuinely stresses the body. We jade our taste buds with over-processed and saturated fatty foods. Our bodies are meant to be nourished with fruits, vegetables, grains and beans that work in harmony with our body. If we eat foods that are full of chemicals, parasites and potential diseases, is it any wonder that we are stressed out internally? It takes a lot of energy to eliminate these substances; and that makes you tired.

Another way to lend a helping hand to a healthier body is to try to eat very light, simple meals in the evening. Before the invention of the light bulb, most people ate just before sundown. In fact, in many societies a golden rule of health is "no food after sundown." If, however, you are forced into eating a meal after sundown, then eat very small portions. It is very debilitating for the health of your body to have to digest a huge meal while you are sleeping.

Another scourge of the modern era is the elimination of the catnap in the afternoon. Eight hours after you wake up, your body physiologically craves a nap. Not a long nap—just fifteen to twenty minutes. But what a difference this makes! It rejuvenates you physically and mentally. Various studies have shown that your physical and mental acuity improves between 40-80% after a 15-20 minute catnap. It is tough to quantify exactly how much someone would improve, but there is no question that it is very beneficial both to your short-term performance and your long-term well-being. Learn to take a nap every afternoon. Note: Don't forget to get permission from your boss first.

One more thought on the catnap. It's an irony of life that we literally have to force young children, who are full of boundless energy, to take a nap in kindergarten; yet when they are in high school and desperately needing to take a nap, they would be sent to the principal's office if they dozed off in the afternoon. The teenage years are ones of significant growth. When the body is growing, it needs extra sleep; for some reason our society seems to discourage that and pass off the craving for sleep as laziness.

It is also essential to block out some quiet time each day . . . our life is so focused on activity. Most of us live with our eyes on the clock. Think about it. When was the last time you treated yourself to a luxurious bath? When was the last time you just sat in a chair? No TV, no noise—nothing. Just you and yourself. To improve the quality of our health, it's important that we go into silence for a short period of time every day.

Recently, the age-old tradition of meditation has found its way to mainstream Western society. The Eastern world has always known the value and importance of meditation. Yet for some reason the Western world considered it too "far out." Meditation is simply the process of getting above the mind in order to reach a state of peacefulness. Some people look at meditation as reaching the state of thinking about "nothing." That is impossible. The mind is never at rest. On the average, we have ten thousand random thoughts per day. That is about seven per minute. True meditation means having a mantra or sound vibration that allows you to get into a state of calmness. If you can't find fifteen minutes a day to meditate or have quiet time, you're just working too hard. It's amazing how we find time to eat three times a day, yet we make excuses about not being able to have fifteen minutes of peaceful repose. Put it in your calendar or in your daily planner, just as you do with your meetings and appointments.

Breathing is also important. Notice how you breathe. Most of you will be taking short breaths . . . mimicking your fast-paced existence. Focus on it now. Take long, deep breaths. Exhale slowly and fully. Do this just ten times and you will notice that your body will be much more relaxed. Proper breathing is one of the most overlooked aspects of our health.

Many people think that today's existence is more stressful than ever before. That's not necessarily true. There has always been stress. There always will be stress. What we don't have today are the mechanisms to relieve them. Plus, we add onto our stress unnecessarily. Let's look at the day of an average person in the fast-paced Western world and see how the stress builds up with virtually no counterbalance.

Stage 1: We wake up and turn on the news so we can get assaulted by the latest round of murders, robberies, arson and other violent acts. Your day in an increasingly violent society has just begun.

Stage 2: We have been deluged with misinformation from corporations who want to make big money on breakfast foods and by doctors who have had virtually no training in nutrition, so we have a big breakfast. We have neglected to realize that breakfast means "break the fast." More stress internally.

Stage 3: We get in our cars. We get caught in traffic jams. Our stress barometer rises. We smile at the person in the car next to us. They look away immediately. Our small attempt at friendliness is rebuffed.

Stage 4: We get to work. Twenty years ago you had the phone and the mail to deal with. Now you have faxes, FedEx and e-mail that hit you upon arrival.

Stage 5: Your bosses have been on a similar stressway as you. Their stress experience often becomes yours.

Stage 6: Your customers are more discriminating. And they want more "instantly."

Stage 7: Time for lunch. Not really time, but you are hungry. So you become another person caught in the web of fast food. You are no longer part of a society that once knew that our best digestion capabilities are between 12 noon and 2 pm. This is when we should eat our biggest meal...slowly. Instead we wolf down a high-fat, high-cholesterol meal which sludges our blood so much that our productivity in the afternoon is slowed down to the point that our most focused attention is toward the waiting to go home. Yet we have work to do and people to see. Our body wants a rest, our mind is on overload yet we keep going.

Stage 8: When the longest, toughest part of the day is finally over you get into your car and get back on the road with all the other people wondering if this is the way to live.

Stage 9: You arrive home and guess what? More stress. More anxiety. You want to be a good listener and hear the family's trials and tribulations of the day. Yet your mind needs a break from the e-mails, employees and customers that bombarded you all day long. You know your body is built to exercise and you would like to give it a workout but that would take away from your family time. Besides, you don't really feel like exercising anyway, so you have a drink instead.

Stage 10: Although you read recently that it is not healthy to eat a big dinner and that you should not eat late, you do it anyway because you are hungry for a good meal. Fast food may have tasted good but it probably wasn't good for you—and deep down you know it.

Stage 11: After dinner you sit down in front of the TV and watch shows that cause your blood pressure and heart rate to go up and your hormone levels to rise.

Stage 12: And so you come full circle—you finish the day as you began: watching the evening news.

Think back on the day. You were in chronic stress. You assaulted your body and your head feels like it was in a washing machine. Most of your day was spent in a theater of conflict. If you look at your health like a bank account, you will see that you spent almost the entire day "drawing upon" your health account. Virtually no deposits were made. And eventually your body breaks down.

If you are to improve your life, health has to be a top priority. Begin by putting the following in your daily routine:

1) Exercise

2) Eating low-fat, high-fiber, low-cholesterol foods
3) Meditation or quiet time (15-30 minutes a day)
4) Focus on slow, relaxed breathing (at home and at work)
5) Take a catnap in the early afternoon. Remember to get your boss's permission.

Whenever you see someone who has truly improved the landscape of their life, almost always one of the key ingredients has been a significant shift in their health style—whether it be exercising more or changing their eating habits. When you are healthy, you have a much better grip on life. This breeds confidence which, in turn, allows you to change and grow more easily.

Chapter Three

Develop a Terrific Attitude

Attitude is the single most determining factor as to whether your life will have meaning and whether you will improve yourself. Employers today are constantly searching for people with good attitudes. Developing or maintaining a terrific attitude will go a long way in improving the landscape of your life. Attitude is much more important than education. In fact, it would be very beneficial if every educational institution would have a class simply titled "Attitude".

We have a choice every day regarding the attitude we will embrace for that day. This is the greatest freedom we have: the freedom to choose our attitude.

Life is full of worries, anxieties, problems, trials, etc....Hard knocks come to everyone. Everybody wakes up every morning with something wrong or something we can complain about. It's not so much what happens to us; it's how we deal with what happens to us. We are all in some sort of prison—some of us look out from behind the bars and see the moon and stars, and others see only mud.

How often have you heard people say "Why me?" or "It's just not my day?" There is no question we cannot direct the wind, but we can adjust the sails of our life. It's interesting to note that things turn out best for those that make the best of the way things turn out.

I suggested having a class in school called Attitude. The biggest challenge would be to define it, because there are so many variables. Although an exact, concise definition may be illusory, there are certain characteristics that people who have a good attitude portray. They are respect, appreciation and sharing.

False pride, and the consequent loss of giving respect, is one of the scourges of our modern world. A person with a good attitude is very respectful. He respects other people's opinions, feelings and cultures. Perhaps the eternal challenge that all societies face is the need to develop the utmost respect for life. We are living in a world where respect for another entity's life has been greatly diminished. One of the most overlooked links to violence in a person is their lack of respect for all life, not just human life. The FBI has known for years that childhood cruelty towards animals is one of the best predictors of a person later being violent towards humans. Most mass-killers had the practice of torturing animals when they were younger.

And what about our slaughterhouses? Most people have never ventured inside one. They don't want to know the origin of the suffering that went into their cellophane-packaged meal that sits on the supermarket counters. When I made my first and only visit to a slaughterhouse, I was shocked that I had spent twenty-five years of my life being totally oblivious to this violent world inside four windowless walls. I remember feeling very disappointed in myself that I hadn't made the connection sooner. Even though I loved the taste of meat and chicken, I have never eaten them since, as I could not justify a lack of respect for those lives. When one comes to respect the lives of all creatures, there is an even greater increase in your respect and appreciation for human life. People fail to respect animals as conscious entities with the right to live out their normal span of life. I love the phrase "teaching a child not to step on a caterpillar is as valuable to the child as it is to the caterpillar."

Appreciation is another pillar of someone with a good attitude. If you want to be happy, make your life a series of experiences of gratitude. When people say "thank you," you can feel the warmth in their appreciation. When they look at a beautiful garden, a sunset, or a full moon, you can sense the enjoyment they get from these simple yet wondrous pleasures of sight.

Today, because of our instant-gratification thought processes, we have become a society of people who expect things rather than appreciate them—particularly in the Western world, where everything is so readily available. For example, we expect water to flow out of a tap, the electricity to go on when we flip a switch and the car to start when we turn on the ignition. It is only when these things do not work that we start to appreciate how we had taken them for granted. As a young player on the professional tennis tour, I stayed with a family in India who told me that the key to happiness was to stop expecting things and simply appreciate what comes your way. If you don't expect things, you won't be disappointed. This was another valuable life lesson.

In Australia, some of the Aboriginal tribes thought it strange that when the missionaries first came they told them to take two minutes before each meal to say grace and express their appreciation to God. The reason they found this strange was that they already appreciated everything that came their way every day, not just at mealtime.

Contentment in life depends not so much on having more but, rather, in appreciating what we already have. One of the best presents you can give a child is to have the inner joy of contentment.

To help you develop a higher level of appreciation, get in the habit of keeping a diary and writing down one thing (or more) that you appreciated that day. It could be a kind act from someone, a beautiful row of trees, or a new friendship made.

Then you can go a step further and start showing your appreciation by doing something. If you have been fortunate to have a meal in front of you three times a day all of your life, take some meals to the homeless. If you've watched someone like a teacher, policeman or a volunteer work each day, performing a service with an enthusiastic smile, give them a small present or write a note of appreciation. Or if you see a movie like *Forrest Gump*, which was morally and spiritually uplifting, it should be applauded. Write the film industry or your local papers encouraging more of this. And what about your mother? If you are fortunate that she is still alive, what have you done on YOUR birthday for her? Remember what she went through for you. Births are not pain free. And once you emerged, you weren't independent. Your mother sacrificed an incredible amount of herself, and a show of appreciation would mean a lot. A genuine thank-you note has become a lost art.

As we were preparing for the birth of our first child, I made a decision that she would only have one toy at a time. And when that toy broke or wore out, we would get her a new one. Boy, was I on an unrealistic channel! Grandparents and friends shattered my plan. And I didn't help either by bringing home the "occasional" toy each time I returned from a trip.

And how about her stuffed animals? I remember having one toy stuffed monkey when I was growing up. At last count she had over fifty. And guess what? All but one or two remain in boxes or on shelves. Did we learn with our second daughter? We were a little better . . . she only has about twenty. But she too prefers only one.

But there is an upside to this. We use this overabundance of toys and stuffed animals to develop the third pillar of a good attitude, which is to share. Each year before Christmas, our children give away their possessions that aren't used to those in need. It isn't easy during the "cleaning out" process, but they feel very good when they see the happiness that their generosity brings to other kids. As adults, we make a living by what we receive, but we make our life by what we give away.

The Japanese believe that those who receive good fortune have an obligation to share. That is why the Japanese have hole-in-one insurance. Almost four million golfers in Japan spend more than 210 million dollars a year on policies to guard against a perfect tee shot. In the event their tee-off shot makes the hole, the insurance company will dole out winnings to them and thus they can share with their fellow players.

It is essential that we uproot our selfish desires and start sharing. Leave part of you everywhere you go, whether it be a kind word or a gift. Some people leave nothing behind. It is as if they never existed. Always remember that a candle loses nothing by lighting another candle.

Because so many of us got caught up in the materialistic hoarding of things, we are not generally natural sharers. We are so concerned about the individual that we've abandoned the sense of group, of community, of civilization. In places like villages in India, where families couldn't exist without sharing, we can learn a lot. When one family's cow dies, and they have lost their important source of milk, all the other families share a little of their surplus. This is how most of the world used to live. The attitude towards sharing was an integral part of life in most countries.

Whether you look at a successful corporation, a successful team or a successful family, one of the common denominators will always be the understanding and acceptance of full cooperation.

When a group of kids are playing together, you will often hear parents saying, "Now share your toys." This is nice advice, but often the kids haven't yet really understood what sharing is all about. Yet the understanding of sharing is what will truly make a difference in that child's life.

If you get up each day with the goals of respecting, appreciating and sharing, you will see a huge shift in your attitude. And as a side benefit, you will see an even bigger shift in others' attitudes towards you. The landscape of your life will have improved.

Chapter Four

Build or Develop
A Solid Set of Values

Too many people today are growing up without internal compasses to help them navigate through the seas of moral pollution. Some of our most important values have been lost in the blind pursuit of material comforts. So often this pursuit causes people to put aside their values for financial gain. As you improve the landscape of your life, you cannot compromise your values.

Many people feel bankrupt in terms of understanding the meaning of life; they are adrift without anchors. The anchors and compasses in life are our values. Without them, we have no home port.

If you want to improve your life, you must have a decent set of values. For some reason, many people seem to dig a hole in the back of their mind, throw in much of their value structure and forget about it. Books and articles abound on the moral poverty of our modern society. They say we are raising a bunch of "moral illiterates." It seems as if too many people are following the sign I saw on a Paris elevator which said "Leave your values at the front desk." Values are essential in becoming a better person. They determine your character.

Our company manages tennis facilities around the world. One of the off-shoots of our tennis program was that we wanted to donate free tennis lessons to people less fortunate or in need of something positive in their lives. One segment we chose to serve was the prison population of Honolulu. We introduced the sport of tennis and it was an instant success. For me personally, the reward was getting to know the prisoners. What surprised me was how nice so many of them were. Many had a very strong set of values. And as many of you know, the prison code is often stronger than the code in the outside world. So what does this mean? Where did these people go astray? Did they lose their moral compass? Yes and no. Everybody has a value structure. What happens is they shape it to THEIR interests rather than the interests of society. They become selfish, and selfishness often overrides their intelligence and their heart. As well, criminals often don't value themselves and, consequently, are incapable of valuing others.

Values should be non-negotiable. Values and ethics are becoming an integral part of corporate training programs globally. Experience has taught us that without moral authority built into the structure of our life, our life will be in chaos. In 1980, the Ethics Resource Center, in Washington DC, could only find seven companies which offered ethics training courses for their workers. In 1997, over 50% of corporations offer this as part of their training program.

A big void in helping to insure that our value structure becomes strong is the lack of role models or heroes. Every day in the media it seems that one of our athletic heroes, political favorites, or supposedly esteemed business leaders is exposed for lack of integrity. The ancient Greeks believed that a great athlete must inevitably be a hero, but these days our sports pages are filled with the news of "falling stars." And each successive government in most countries seems to have leaders who have failed the people they are supposed to have served because their value judgment went astray. In many cases, they became poll obsessed and afraid to take a stand. They choose what is popular rather than what is right. And in the business world, economic interests almost always take precedence over moral concerns. Far too often in the business world, people try to change the score after the deal is made. Once upon a time you could do business on a handshake, trusting that a man's word was his bond.

Moral growth is not possible without the discipline of regular, personal reflection. Think about how many times recently you have compromised your values and principles. And when you start compromising on one thing, you compromise on many. Your values should be non-negotiable. And your values should be reflected in the way you live. Moral courage means the courage to be moral. And as William Bennet puts it: "There is nothing more influential in a child's life than the moral power of quiet example."

So how does one go about building a solid set of values? Sometimes this can be difficult, because our values are often left up to personal interpretations. But try talking to ten individuals from different religious or spiritual persuasions. What you will find is that there is a common set of denominators that weaves throughout each set of guidelines from these various doctrines or scriptures.

It has been interesting to note that so many wars and conflicts are based on religious or scriptural differences or misinterpretations. In spite of the fact that about 98% of the world's major religions talk about the same message, we seem to focus on the 2% of differences.

A second exercise to aid you in developing a good set of values is to keep a little diary of the qualities of the best people with whom you've interacted. You will also find that they have a common set of values.

As I have traveled to 134 countries, it is easy to look at the superficial differences in the various countries and races. However, deep down we're pretty much the same in our heart; and if we do a little homework, it is quite easy to come up with a good set of values that will enable us to enhance the landscape of our life.

Values are values . . . period. They do not begin or end with a certain age or era. Too many parents have a different value structure from what they want their children to have. Too many leaders in the business or government world have a different value structure from the people by whom they are entrusted to lead. You should live your life in such a way so that when your children or your friends think of integrity and a high-value structure, they will think of you.

Chapter Five

Take Responsibility for Your Life and Your Actions

Anyone who watches the daytime talk shows in America has come to see that whining has become our national pasttime and entertainment. It has become a national orgy of whining and self-pity. As the late Chicago Tribune columnist Mike Rokyo said, "Americans sit slack-jawed while catching their daily dose of weirdos on the daily tell-all freak shows. Listening to these people who have chosen to expose the sordid details of their personal lives to the world confirms that we have abused our freedom." I'm not a big fan of most of the daytime talk shows, but if you want to get a sense of what Mr. Rokyo means, spend an afternoon watching these shows.

A free society carries with it responsibility—responsibility to ourselves, to our family, to our friends, to our community, to our country and to our world.

In talking with prisoners throughout the United States, I was amazed at how few of them take personal responsibility for their actions. They blame their plight on their parents, their aunts and uncles, their grandparents, their brothers and sisters, their teachers, their friends, their environment, society and even the government. Very few had the courage or the moral integrity to say, "I did it. I messed up. I am in prison because it was I who made the wrong choice. No one else is to blame." If only they could see that with choices comes responsibility and that we must accept the consequences of those choices.

We have to stop looking for excuses. We have all seen very successful, forthright individuals rise out of horrific poverty and an abusive family. And we have seen individuals who have a loving family and a wonderful material existence go off the deep end and commit hideous acts. In the end, the buck stops with us and we must terminate our search to place the blame elsewhere.

Once we come to grips with the fact that we are the pillar of our destiny and that we build it ourselves, then we can turn our sense of responsibility outwards.

Take our athlete today who is highly compensated for playing a sport. They take on celebrity status. They are heroes to many young kids. Yet this pampered world in which they live often brings out the worst in their nature. They get paid three million dollars a year to hit a little ball or put a bigger ball in a hoop and they can't take five seconds to sign an autograph for the kid to whom they are a hero. They reject their responsibility to the public who pays their check.

Or what about the person who wants a raise and more benefits but in return wants less work? More and more people want shorter work hours and more pay, and in many cases the quality of the work does not match up with the amount paid. Nowadays, achieving a better life through hard work is being replaced by the excuse mill. If you want to improve the landscape of your life, it is a good idea to build a good work ethic, admit your mistakes and learn from them so that you can be better tomorrow than you were today.

Consider parents who bring a child into the world and then abandon their responsibility to do everything in their power and capabilities to make certain that that child has a decent life. They may not be able to give the child a lot of material comfort but they can always give the most important comforts . . . those from the heart. Children won't always remember the toys they had, but they will always remember the hugs.

Our family lives in Hawaii and a while ago I had a chance to hear Ninoa Thompson speak. He is one of only a couple of individuals in the world who has learned a certain art of celestial navigation. When he and his crew re-enacted the original Polynesian voyage between Tahiti and Hawaii, they did so without any modern navigational techniques. At sea for many weeks at a time, Ninoa said, "I don't sleep. It's part of my responsibility." He saw the lives of others as way more important than his sleep.

And how about our world? With 5.3 billion people (and rising), what is our responsibility? Can our little effort to be responsible make a difference? Absolutely. Remember that a deed well done never stops with you. Your example is passed on and on and on. Think of all the wonderful inventions, products and ideas. Almost every one began with one person.

Before bringing this chapter to a close, I would like to ask a question. Do you believe that this is your one and only life? Or do you believe that you've existed before and will have another life? Depending upon which poll you look at, in America, those who believe that we have had and will have other lives ranges between 52% and 72%. Whatever viewpoint or feeling you have, let's assume that we will have another life. Can you imagine if the whole world believed we were coming back again? I tend to think that the level of responsibility would go way up.

Our American Indians used to say, "Make a decision based on six generations from now." Many people today base their decisions on six minutes from now. If you knew you were coming back, it would make you much more responsible. It might make you realize that your actions, thoughts and words will have consequences in this life and in the future.

In Eastern religion, the law of karma (for every action there is an equal and opposite reaction) is part of the doctrine. In the Bible, the comparable instruction is "As you sow, so shall you reap." If only we could take these two simple guidelines and incorporate them into our lives in everything we do. And if you don't believe you are coming back here, try to leave the place a little nicer because you had the personal courage to take your responsibility of living seriously.

Chapter Six

Chapter Six

Get Out of Your Comfort Zone

When you talk to people on their deathbed, very few regret what they've done. Almost all regret what they HAVEN'T done. And when you explore further, most of these people had become trapped in their comfort zones. Although their physical bodies were about to give out, they had actually died many years earlier as their comfort zones became their coffins.

When people transition from school into the working world, they are told that they are now going into "the real world." And they go into the real world and work real hard, but they get so busy making a living that they forget to make a life. For many, work is something you do 8-10 hours a day so you can buy more toys. It is very important that one realizes that good, hard work is in itself a noble enterprise.

The problem is most people don't like their jobs; or if they like their jobs, they aren't challenged. Rare is the person that loves their job. And rare is the person who is in a job that they love that is genuinely making a positive difference in people's lives. And seldom do these two pluses combine with the opportunity to learn more every day. Therefore, everyone must go beyond their jobs to get out of the comfort zone.

What is the comfort zone? It is simply the imaginary box of your life, outside of which you don't dare venture for fear of feeling or being uncomfortable. Getting out of the comfort zone can be as small as trying an entirely new cuisine that you've never tasted before—all the way to someone who is terrified of heights learning to skydive. But, ultimately, the best venture outside of the comfort zone is to do something that will benefit others.

How about flying to India for a month and helping the late Mother Theresa's Sisters of Charity Foundation take care of those sick people who can't afford their next meal? Don't take your checkbook . . . take your heart. Or how about studying how important our rainforests are and helping to stop the mass destruction of these precious ecosystems? Or how about writing an inspiring script, instead of something like one of today's movies, which just flash images of violence, sex and crime our way?

Getting out of your comfort zone means you can become a human lighthouse for someone else. You shouldn't be afraid to take a risk or be criticized for venturing out of your zone. New information and new ideas upset lazy minds. You should have a curiosity to explore life and learn. Make your life into a tunnel of wonderment and discovery. A creative life is a continual quest. Remember that most people are in a comfort zone and your getting out of it will make them feel guilty. And remember it's not what you get out of the process materially, it's what you become internally.

The United States of America has a volume of problems. Many nations now do many things better than we do. But one thing that America is still tops in is the opportunity to dream, to explore, to adventure and to get out of the comfort zone. It is a country where many dreams have come true. And as writer

Dan Millman said, "Dreams are the children of our soul."

We are a country where millions of dreams have become reality. Our part of the world is full of the stories of people who arrive from foreign lands with little more than a few personal possessions and make a successful life, even by the standards of their new home. And how many Americans, because of the numerous opportunities at home, have been able to explore the world?

There are three types of people: those who work all day (and seldom get out of their comfort zone); those who dream all day (and seldom have any zone to get into); and those who work, yet dream thirty to sixty minutes per day. It is usually the latter group that gets out of their comfort zone to make a difference in their life as well as the lives of others.

I remember in June 1996, being in Fiji with Ananda Madhawan, the chef at the resort where we vacation each year. He had just developed a passion for golf and decided to build a golf course. In America, we have high-paid golf designers supported by high-paid landscapers. I asked him what his budget was. He didn't have any. And who did he have in mind to design it? "Oh, I will," he replied. Whoever heard of a chef designing a golf course? Let alone an individual who started playing golf two months earlier. Talk about getting out of your comfort zone!

Yet, on July 12, 1997, the Prime Minister of Fiji officially opened the nine-hole golf course on this tiny island in the Pacific that doesn't even allow cars on it. No blue prints, no designers, no architects, no land-planners . . . just a vision of what it would look like in Ananda's head. Thirteen months after our first trip to the back of the island, the course looked just like he had described it to me a year earlier. Ananda works very hard (six to seven days a week), yet he took time to dream each day and get out of his comfort zone.

If you focus on growth, you will generally have more peace of mind than those who are seeking happiness through a comfortable life. It is always good to have something to look forward to.

When you get accustomed to exiting the comfort zone, you will see that life is a series of endless opportunities. You become much more positive. You are more confident because you see that you are making progress. You are much more aware. You aren't just watching things happen . . . you are making things happen. Opportunities don't go unnoticed—because you are alert. This is why the next time I see a photograph of a picture of a starving baby, I'll hope the photographer got out of the comfort zone, put the camera down and fed the baby.

One final thought on getting out of your comfort zone: Think about the people who will be affected by your transition. Remember to close the door properly. Very few people realize that closing the door on a chapter of your life is just as important as opening the next door.

Look at how nice people are in their first interview for a job. It's often been said that the best you will ever see someone is on the day of their first interview with you. They're usually polite, respectful, flexible, etc. Yet look at how they act upon departure from that job. They don't honor the term of their contract and the quality of their work usually dips dramatically in their last few weeks. People have to remember that closing the old door carefully is just as important as opening the new one. In order to improve the landscape of your life, it's important that you realize that each job you have is a building block in the construction of your life. Don't leave any weaknesses in the structure.

Getting out of your comfort zone doesn't have to happen today. The decision can be made today, but before the final transition, write down the names of all the people who will be affected by this change. And figure out the most polite, respectful way of making it comfortable for them as well. If you do this, most everybody will be on the sidelines cheering for you to succeed in your efforts to improve the landscape of your life.

Chapter Seven

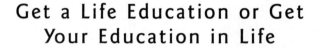

Get a Life Education or Get Your Education in Life

I find it very ironic that in our modern educational system an athletic coach at a university can be fired for his team's poor performance, yet a professor at that same university who performs poorly cannot usually be fired. It seems strange that an institution of higher education places more importance on the performance of a coach than a teacher. If you look at most people who have improved the landscape of their life, it usually came AFTER they finished their formal education.

I'm not sure why I'm not very supportive of our modern educational system as it is today. Perhaps I'm not so supportive of formal schooling because I wasn't a very good student. I spent most of my time struggling. But one of the best educations in life is the one gotten by struggling. So I should be appreciative of the fact that I wasn't a good student.

Perhaps it's because school sharpens the brain but neglects the heart. Education of the heart is more important than anything else. We are falling short of exposing students to values. We must realize that wisdom comes from living, not just from studying.

Perhaps it's because I look back on school and realize that the millions of facts I learned were of little to no value in my later life. But then again maybe I should appreciate the process rather than the result of having millions of useless facts stored somewhere in my brain.

Perhaps it's because we're falling short in exposing students to what is really important in life. We need classes in character, values, leadership, empathy, discipline and respect. We need to teach students what is actually important.

Perhaps it's because I've personally interviewed over ten thousand people for positions in our company and a large percentage of them don't have any people skills . . . skills that are essential for them to deal with the public.

Perhaps it's because I've listened to psychiatrists petition to get mandatory physical education out of the schools because the classes have competition in them and they say that competition is bad for the students. And forty-nine of our fifty states complied. What are they saying? Life is a competition. Competition comes from the Latin word *competere*, meaning to strive or come together. Perhaps it's because I have realized how confining it is to force people to sit for such extended periods. It's not healthy mentally, physically or emotionally. The body is built to move. As well, if a physical education class is run properly the students can learn a lot about cooperation. Whether it is an athletic team, a corporation or a family, the level of success is always much higher if there is strong cooperation among everyone.

Perhaps it's because I have seen what teachers today have to go through. I speak to a lot of teachers' groups. When I ask what their two principal concerns are, they mention a lack of enthusiasm from the students and, secondly, the level of violence possessing them. Teachers aren't paid enough for what they have to go through.

Perhaps it's because I get tired of hearing how parents won't support the teachers in their disciplinary efforts. Our educational institutions can't be free to instill a high level of respect where parents are going to second guess their efforts. I'm one of those that feels very fortunate to have grown up within a system where teachers had the liberty to strap an unruly student. I learned quickly and it helped. Even though I'm a deeply nonviolent person, this is one area where I appreciate its use. I'm not advocating a return to corporal punishment, which has definitely lost favor over the last two or three decades. What I do know is that in the past 30 years of speaking at schools, the level of discipline seems to be decreasing each year.

Whatever the case, the most important education in life is the one where we learn about life itself and its purpose. True wisdom comes more from living than from studying. I recently saw a photo in a magazine. It had a father holding up his young son and they were looking at one another. Underneath it said, "If a father can't tell his son what the purpose of life is, then his own life is a failure." It made you think about what really is important. After reading that article, I put together a simple statement of the purpose of life for my seven-year-old daughter: "To be compassionate, to serve other people and to be humble."

She, like her dad, is struggling in school as I write this. We will do all we can to get her grades up so she will feel confident among peers. But I'm not really worried; because I know if she learns this simple mission statement of her purpose of life, she will do quite well. As she lives her life, it isn't going to be very important in the big picture whether she got an A, B or C in Grade 1. But it will be very rewarding to her as she lives her life to practice humility, compassion and service.

Those who live close to the land often have the best life education. And their inner wisdom often dwarfs that of the average city folk in their knowledge of life. A wonderful example are the Aborigines in Australia and their philosophy on growth, learning and education. They consider our celebration of birthdays a little strange. They do not see why we should celebrate something that just happens. We don't do any work to get older and after twenty-one there's usually nothing to celebrate. The Aborigines have days of celebration throughout the year but they are when someone has mastered a skill or increased their knowledge or grown spiritually. They know themselves when they have improved and they call for the day of celebration. It is not an egotistical endeavor, just something to celebrate. What a nice tradition. We should all celebrate our successes, not just a day we added another year to our life.

Can you imagine how different the world would be if we celebrated the days when people actually grew and accomplished something in their life education? Then Louis Armstrong's song "Oh What a Wonderful World" would have a lot more relevance.

One of the questions I asked leaders when I interviewed them for a book I wrote about leadership and service was "What is more important, logic or intuition?" Virtually everyone said intuition. Yet when I ask new college graduates this question, most say "logic."

What this shows is that modern education teaches logic and life education teaches intuition. Intuition is like a muscle. The more you use it, the stronger it becomes. There is no question that sometimes you need to use your head in making decisions, but most of the time the answers are in our heart.

One of the best ways to increase our intuitive abilities is to have hands-on experience. It is worth noting that young kids in school get a lot of field trips or educational experiences outside of the classroom. Rare are the schools that do this for the older students, those who are getting close to having to make real-life decisions in real-life situations. Our hearts get opened most by hearing and seeing.

I've often thought that the ideal education would be one that would blend scholastics (accumulation of knowledge) with the spirit of service and compassion for all life. Maybe it's a little too idealistic, but we know that we can't stick to our current path. When one goes to schools today, rare is the smile. There just aren't many excited students who truly enjoy learning. And if we don't enjoy learning and respect education, we definitely can't improve our life.

Chapter Eight

Build Protective Shields

All living entities have some protection against outside intruders. Modern people's idea of protection is to barricade themselves at night with chain locks, dead-bolts, guns and alarms. It has become a world where fear abounds in many places.

Fear can be eliminated by knowledge or by faith. For example, if you walk into your home at night and hear noises in another room, your heart starts beating faster because you think someone is in your house. Yet when you turn on all the lights and check things out and realize that it was only the wind, you relax and your pulse returns to normal. What happened? Knowledge eliminated the fear.

And faith is also very helpful in alleviating fear. Over the years I've met certain individuals who say they don't have any faith. My next question to them is: "When was the last time you were on an airplane?" When they tell me when last they took a flight, I ask them what the name of the pilot was. Obviously they don't remember it, and my comment to them is: "You mean to say you put your life in the hands of someone you don't even know?" We all have faith in something, even if it was the pilot on our last airplane flight.

If we're going to improve ourselves, we must have protective shields. If you want to change yourself or your situation, there will inevitably be naysayers who will challenge you, question you, doubt you. What will help you more than anything is to have a commitment to your improvement that is so strong that no outside influence can alter your plans.

If you listen to the stories of people who have done some incredible things, all of them will mention people who said "they couldn't do it." How did they block this pessimism out? They had shields to protect them.

Let's say you wanted to change your eating habits from being a staunch meat eater to a vegetarian. Your first year will be full of people questioning your sanity. People will tell you you're going to get sick and maybe die. They worry about you getting enough protein. They think you will be malnutritioned. Suddenly, all those friends and family members who don't know the difference between a heart-attack and a stroke are offering you medical advice. How do you handle this change? You get the appropriate knowledge and with this knowledge you can explain to them not only what you are doing but also why you are doing it.

And because you yourself have the knowledge, you won't be fearful or doubt your decision. You are protected. Before any life style change, make sure you have researched enough to the point where no one can derail you. It is also helpful to understand why people don't want you to change. It's very simple. Change frightens many people and by your actions you are forcing them to THINK about change. Just as we change clothes when we change climates, so must we change our protective mechanisms.

In addition to having knowledge about where you are headed, it is essential that you believe you will get there. You can't hope.

You know. No question. You may fail, but the failure wasn't due to any doubt.

Many people have failed in their endeavors to improve themselves because they weren't protected along the way. They had no idea that they would be attacked. If you set out on your path to improvement, wear your invisible suit of armor. You wouldn't think of going out on an adventurous trip to the North Pole without lots of cold-weather clothes or going to sleep out in the Amazon jungle without a mosquito net.

In 1987, a major general, Sitiveni Rabuka, staged a military coup in Fiji. It was a physically non-violent coup yet highly controversial. Major General Sitiveni Rabuka became Prime Minister. For ten years the country struggled politically and economically. For ten years he received a multitude of commendations and criticisms. Parliamentary debates sometimes turned into vicious attacks on Prime Minister Rabuka.

One day while having lunch with him, I asked him how he handled this. His answer was a simple yet thoughtful one. He said, "Before any parliamentary session I prepare myself mentally and spiritually. I know that I will often be verbally attacked. But I am prepared for it. Having been in the military for many years definitely prepared me for being shot at." Prime Minister Rabuka had his protective shield on.

There's no question that one of the principal reasons people don't complete their journey of change or improvement in life is that they weren't protected.

Chapter Nine

Commune with Nature

In the last one hundred years we have evolved from the rhythms of nature to the rhythms of the electronic age. We've been on a rapid retreat from nature. We listen to too much TV, radio, ringing telephones, etc., and far too little to nature. Year by year the number of people with first-hand experience on the land dwindles. Healthy humans innately have a deep spiritual connection to the environment and to lose this is not a positive step forward.

If you want to change the landscape of your life, one of your priorities is to reconnect with nature. We must try to ease ourselves out of the concrete jungles that have enveloped our existence. We need to seek out places where we can regenerate our nerves that have been jangled by the din of man-made noises. Nature plays a vital role in uplifting us physiologically, physically and emotionally. Nature awakens something inside of us. When people dream of a better life, they don't think of tall concrete buildings, traffic jams, polluted air or noisy streets. They think of mountain streams, oceans, lakes, forests and beaches. Water is very soothing. Sitting and watching a stream go by can do wonders for your spirit. Even in the center of cities, the greatest asset is the water fountain. Watch how many people gather around it in the Spring and Summer. The soothing effects of water in any form helps take the edge off our daily troubles.

Improving the Landscape of Your Life

Many people in industrialized countries find their life to be spiritually hollow, devoid of a natural environment. Wilderness awakens our spirit. We should do everything possible to increase our time spent communing with nature.

Another big plus that will come from our communion with nature will be an awareness of how much disregard there has been for our ecology. We have caused more ecological damage in the past century than all thousand previous generations put together. Although there are small segments of the population who do not accepts this, all one has to do is compare the earth, water and air to 100 years ago. As we look at people with masks on their face because of polluted air in the cities, to the huge volumes of sales on bottled water as opposed to taking fresh, clean water from underground, to the pollution of our topsoil globally—it is easy to see the massive destruction that has taken place. Our major desire for material acquisitions has resulted in our permanently altering our land, water and air. Our rivers have become like sewers, and the EPA in America reports that 40% of the fresh water is unsafe for swimming now.

The ecological crisis is a crisis of values. The world's developing countries are tending to let industrial progress take over their economies, oblivious to environmental destruction. It has only been in the last fifteen to twenty years that the world has become aware of how important the rainforests are to everybody. We need to commune more with nature so we can learn how everything is interconnected. We must be part of putting nature back to a position of importance rather than relegating her as just another trash heap.

Far too many people today grow up without the sounds of nature. The closest they come to nature is when they go to their local music store and buy sounds of nature reproduced on an audio cassette. In fact, the popularity of these tapes is an indication of how much we appreciate the sounds of nature.

Recently we had a chance to spend time with two families immediately after they returned from vacation. Both had been gone for two weeks. One family had gone on a ten-city tour of Europe visiting historical landmarks. Eleven airports, four train stations, three rental cars and four buses later, they returned home exhausted. They had seen some beautiful historical architecture and woven together pieces of their history classes in school, but they were "wiped out." They had only "communed" with man-made accomplishments. And they needed a second vacation to recover from the first one.

The other couple had gone on a camping trip. They had escaped civilization for the entire time. They didn't even take a radio or tape recorder. We saw them the day they returned. There was a calmness about them. They looked healthy and were truly recharged. Communing with nature does that to you. You are emotionally and spiritually charged when you spend time in a natural setting.

Even at the South Pole in Antarctica at McMurdo Station, plants play a major role. At the station they have a hydroponics building (a hundred meters full of lettuce, tomatoes, squash and other plants), all illuminated by artificial light. People become depressed with the long, harsh winters there, yet a few hours a day with the plants does wonders for the morale of the residents.

Unfortunately, our connection to the animal world is limited as well. Yet the fact that our zoos are the most popular attraction in almost every country is an indication of how much we appreciate them as well. Recognizing animals as our moral equivalent will help nature take a giant leap forward in terms of our respect. All human beings are born with a lifeline connected to other living beings.

If you wish to improve your life, set aside a portion of your day or week to visit nature. You can simplify, coexist and increase your appreciation of the wonderment of it all. You can use it as the chance to dream or create. Or you can use it to increase your commitment to help it heal. Whatever the case, you will feel better afterwards. As the poet Cowper said, "God made the country, and man made the town."

Chapter Ten

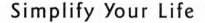

Simplify Your Life

There once was a yogi who sat on a mountaintop meditating on a simple straw mat. However, a rat kept nibbling at his toes and disturbing his tranquillity of thought. So he went and got a cat to keep away the rat. However, the cat was hungry and needed milk. So he went and got a cow to feed the cat who was keeping away the rat. But his meditation time was being decreased by having to milk the cow, so he decided he better get a wife who could take care of the milking of the cow. But the wife was very unhappy for she wanted a place to live in, so in order to get money to build a house he went out and got a job. You can finish the story anyway you want, but it points out how our lives can get more and more complicated.

Recently a Time/CNN poll showed that 79% of Americans wanted to simplify their life. Nowhere is this more evident than when you look at the voluntary simplicity movement that is sweeping America and many other countries globally. They want simpler, gentler life styles but feel caught in a whirlpool and don't know the way out. Too many people have tried to get a life style instead of a life. They've got a civil war going on in their head and things are getting more and more complicated. We live in a state of almost constant distraction. So, if you're going to simplify the landscape of your life, where do you begin?

Well, let's start with your possessions. Think how many clothes are in your closet that you just don't wear. A trip to Goodwill or The Salvation Army will benefit you and the recipients of some of your wardrobe. Then look in each room of your house. How many "things" do you have that have no function or sentimental value whatsoever. They just sit there. Can you part with them? If you are on the road to simplifying your life, you bet you can. And don't forget your storage areas and garage if you have them. It's time to say good-bye to so many of those items that you will never ever use for the rest of your life.

Now let's look at your food choices. How much is thrown out? How many items are in your freezer or in the cupboards that have been there for so long? There are a lot of hungry people who would appreciate your generosity. And how about the size of your meals? If you take both of your hands in an open, cupping fashion and join them together, that is the volume of food your stomach can comfortably handle in one sitting. Look at the healthiest people in the world. They eat simple meals built around beans, rice, grains or noodles. Our food choices in the Western world are so complex and overtaxing on the body that we have spawned all kinds of life style diseases like cancer, osteoporosis and heart attacks. We're the only species that eats more than we need.

And how about fasting every seven to ten days for twenty-four hours? Anyone who has ever fasted for the first time usually experiences a feeling of being weak or sometimes dizzy. Part of the reason is that they are going through a detoxification process. However, once one gets comfortable with the understanding and practicality of a fast such an individual joins those who have experienced the huge physical, emotional, spiritual and even economic benefits of the process. If you are going to fast for the first time, I would recommend a juice fast; there is very little energy required to digest juices, so the majority of your energy can go to the healing processes occurring within your body. The ultimate, ideal fast is just water for the full benefit of cleansing. A word of caution: pregnant women and children should not fast. The process of this austerity helps one spiritually and improves discipline.

Now it's time to go through your weekly schedule. Try to eliminate one thing each day that will move you toward a simpler game plan. Do you really need to have four social functions when three is more adequate? Take that extra night and focus on your family and do something simple. Go for a family picnic or eat in front of the fireplace. Read a book instead of watching TV.

Around the world, cultures are being exposed to the modern world and the innocence of simplicity of their former world is lost forever. A simpler way of life allows us to realize some balance. Yet some people mistake simplicity for ignorance. The real message of simple-heartedness in the movie *Forrest Gump* was misinterpreted by some. But the majority of people were genuinely uplifted by Forrest's innocence.

Have you ever seen a picture of a person at age five and at age fifty? The five-year-old child's face is full of indescribable innocence and the fifty-year-old's face shows all the heavy loads that the body, heart and spirit have carried. One of the most poignant phrases of all time is that which says, "Youth is such a wonderful time; it's too bad it's wasted on the young." The five-year-old's life is very simple, while the fifty-year-old's life is often excruciatingly complex.

It's important to differentiate between simplicity that is consciously chosen or externally imposed. The homeless person on the street may have a very simple existence with minimal clothes, no insurance for a car or home, and no phone or electricity bills. But this situation is usually forced and is not healthy for the soul. Those people, however, who consciously say, "Time's up!"—in terms of their escalating number of possessions and increasing frenetic pace of life—are the ones who can truly improve their life.

Chapter Eleven

Educate Your Heart

Of all the education we get, the education of the heart is the most important. Yet in our modern educational system, this is basically neglected. There is a huge spiritual vacuum at the heart of this country's technological revolution. Without spiritual knowledge, our life is very incomplete. We need a connection to a higher being.

It is important to differentiate here between actual spirituality and religion. Unfortunately, religion seems to instigate violence rather than to eliminate it. Historically, almost every war has had a religious conflict component to it. Spirituality may be defined as the fountainhead and essence of all religion, ethics, morals and values—above and beyond any sectarianism or party spirit.

Our real crisis today is the corruption of our hearts. We fill our bellies with food and our homes with toys and ornaments, but most of us haven't properly nourished our soul.

A great teacher from India illustrated this point with the following analogy: "If the owner of a bird only pays attention to the cage, polishing it very carefully, and neglects the inhabitant of the cage, the bird will die. In the same way, if we simply pay attention to the body, neglecting its inhabitant (the soul), spiritually we will be as good as dead."

Too many people today are simply polishing their "cage."

The two things that seem to most influence the conduct and behavior of individuals are leadership and spiritual teachings. If you want to get your life to another plateau, you need another to be a teacher (leader) and you need to have some spiritual teachings.

How do you know the difference between a true spiritual teacher and someone like a Jim Jones who led his followers to mass suicide in Guyana? It's actually very simple—is the teacher following bona fide spiritual teachings? Pseudo-spiritual leaders give their own interpretations on a scripture. Many change words to ease their conscience and to be able to carry on with their own material enjoyment rather than their spiritual advancement. The true spiritual teacher is not attracted to any material gain for personal use. They will use the material gifts they receive to do more in service. But they don't purchase lots of cars and have multiple sexual relations. Don't accept a teacher blindly. Listen to them. Are their actions in sync with their teachings? That is the most important question.

You don't have to personally meet your teacher but you must meet his or her teachings. I feel that the time will come when there will be a need for a personal, spiritual teacher, just as we have a personal physical fitness trainer.

Educating your heart is one of the biggest steps you can take in improving the landscape of your life. Every person who has really improved themselves has had a spiritual base to return to in times of crisis or challenge.

Billions of dollars each year are spent putting makeup and lotion on our bodies. Yet very few dollars are spent trying to improve and educate our heart. Do a weekly tabulation and total up the hours that you've spent improving (or trying to improve) your body as opposed to the hours spent trying to improve your heart.

It is as if we hope the tree will grow if we water its leaves instead of the root. Our root is our spiritual spark, our heart, our life energy force, our soul. If we focus on that, our lives will take a dramatic turn for the better.

Chapter Twelve

Live Your Life with Humility

Humility is the final achievement in life. Too many people are in illusion and see themselves as the all-important figure in the universe. Nobody likes to be around an egotistical person.

What makes someone egotistical? It's because they are insecure. Great people don't have to tell people they are great. Others do the talking for them.

Humility in someone who achieves greatness is very attractive. In September 1995,

Cal Ripken of the Baltimore Orioles baseball team got a twenty-two minute standing ovation for playing in 2,131 consecutive games. This in itself is not such a big deal; millions of people all over the world have gone to work for 2,131 days in a row, and they didn't have an off-season of four months either. But what made those twenty-two minutes a tear-inducing, goose-bump experience was that Cal Ripken is a high-profile athlete. And he was very humble about his achievement—this was the endearing part of Cal Ripken.

Anymore, the words "humble athlete" simply don't seem to go together. Look at American football after most players cross the goal line for a touchdown. This is self-celebration in its ugliest form. Why not just score, drop the ball and remain humble? (Remember, there were ten other players who helped get them there.) The players should look like they will be back to score many more times—so what's the big deal?

The megabucks showered on these young kids and youthful adults has resulted in a warped value structure for so many of them. I remember talking to a coach in the NBA who said he liked to go to shopping malls to relax on the afternoon before a game on the road. I asked him if any of the players ever joined him. He said, "Oh no, they own everything. There's nothing for them to buy." And owning "things" has become equated with the belief that these individuals are independent and don't owe anything to anybody. Their arrogance is shown in their disdain for the media, interviewers, autograph seekers and anyone else they can't see as someone who can help them.

The late Arthur Ashe received a wonderful phrase of wisdom from his father: "To whom more is given, more is expected." As your material world gets better, you must be humble enough to keep your spiritual growth on an equal path.

For some reason, people, particularly in America, equate humility as a weakness, instead of a strength. We have become attracted to overconfident leaders. And when they fall, our confidence and faith falls with them. In the marathon of life, it is the humble people who are the most highly respected.

The death of Princess Diana forced a lot of people to truly understand what her greatest assets were. Sure, she had a lot of material assets such as beauty, wealth, fame, etc., but in the end what people most appreciated about her was her humility. She was willing to take young children with AIDS, with ragged clothes on their back, and allow them to sit on her knee. It is rather ironic that here is someone who had all of the assets that so many people strive for, yet in the end the world mourned her loss because of who she was. And the foundation of who she was was her humility.

In that same week, one of Princess Diana's heroes, Mother Theresa, passed on. Here was once a young Catholic nun who was teaching high school in Calcutta. Yet she kept looking out the window and seeing lepers on the street and she knew she had to leave the security of her convent and go out and help them. Her only material possessions were her white sari with a blue border and her prayer beads.

Here were two women who were, quite possibly, the most beloved women in the world—and humility was one of their defining qualities.

How can you become more humble? Start by thinking of yourself less and others more. Notice in your next conversation with someone, whether you're the one asking the majority of the questions with a genuine interest in getting an answer. Or are you the one monopolizing the conversation with tales and woes of your life?

And when you accomplish something of note, do you take the place of CNN and let the world know? Or do you humbly and quietly accept the good fortune that has come your way? This doesn't mean that you don't share your success with those closest to you. They can do the PR for you. It's always better when a third party talks about your feats.

And how about your service to others? Do you do it for the reward? Or do you do it in a humble manner with no expectation of accolades? Only then did you do it because it had to get done or because it came from your heart—without any strings attached.

It helps to be aware of how admirable it is to be humble. Start looking for this wonderful quality in people—you will find that they make the best of friends. And anyone who has friends of this stature has to improve his/her life, even if only by osmosis.

Time To Say Good-Bye

In life, it is those who care that genuinely leave something behind. If we can stop taking this gift called life for granted and sincerely make an effort to serve others in a compassionate and humble way, our experiences will be much richer.

At the end of the day as we put our head on the pillow, it is far more rewarding to know that someone's life was better today because of something we did. It is much more gratifying than tallying up all the "things" we bought for ourselves during the day.

Is it worth it to improve the landscape of your life? You bet it is. Ask any gardener or landscaper if they don't look upon their finished product and feel a deep sense of satisfaction. Can you imagine what it is like to look back and say that you were the architect of the improvement of you as a human being? Now, that's rewarding!

The former baseball great Jackie Robinson aptly summed it up when he said, "A life is not important except for the impact it has on others' lives." And while you're at the helm of this thing called life, say a little prayer of thanks for the opportunity to have been able to light the way for someone else.

P.S I finished writing this book in Fiji, where I have done most of my writing over the years. One afternoon my seven-year-old daughter and I were walking along a quiet beach. She noticed a fellow smoking a cigarette. Out of the blue she said, "Daddy, smoking isn't cool. Do you know what's cool? Being cool is becoming a good person." Children really are our teachers.

If you enjoyed this book, we feel sure you will also enjoy Peter Burwash's other titles listed at the back. Take a look now!

Book Order Form

- ☎ Telephone orders: Call 1-888-TORCHLT (1-888-867-2458).
  Have your VISA or MasterCard ready.
- ✳ Fax orders: 559-337-2354
- ✉ Postal orders: Torchlight Publishing, P. O. Box 52,
  Badger, CA 93603-0052, USA

▲ World Wide Web: www.torchlight.com

Please send the following:

The Key to Great Leadership	$11.95 ✕_____	= $_____
Total Health: The Next Level	$11.95 ✕_____	= $_____
Improving the Landscape of Your Life	$12.95 ✕_____	= $_____
	Sales tax: (CA residents add 7.25%)	$_____
	Shipping / handling (see below)	$_____
	TOTAL	$_____

⃝ **Please send me your catalog and info on other books by Torchlight Publishing**

Company_____

Name_____

Address_____

City _____ State_____ Zip_____

(I understand that I may return any books for a full refund—no questions asked.)

Payment:

⃝ Check / money order enclosed   ⃝ VISA   ⃝ MasterCard

Card number_____

Name on card_____ Exp. date_____

Signature_____

Shipping and handling:

Book rate: USA $2.00 for first book, $1.00 for each additional book. Canada: $3.00 for first bo
$2.00 for each additional book. Foreign countries: $4.00 for first book, $3.00 for each additic
book. (Surface shipping may take 3–4 weeks. Foreign orders please allow 6–8 weeks for delive